Table of Contents

Seasons of LOVE

From Heartbreak to Healing,
One Season at a Time

MAMATA SAMPATH

About the Author

Mamata Sampath is an avid reader and writer who discovered her love for storytelling at the age of five, letting her imagination soar through the written word.

Formerly a corporate communications and public relations professional, she now devotes herself fully to writing. *Seasons of Love* is a unique blend of learning from people's life journeys, bits of her personal experiences, and the emotions she draws from reading books and watching movies.

As she dives into stories, both on the page and the screen, Mamata becomes part of the narrative, feeling the characters' joy, pain, and heartbreak as though they were her own. These stories, along with her observations of the world around her, have inspired much of her creative work.

A true empath, Mamata fully immerses herself in every story she encounters. When watching movies, she often finds herself deeply moved, shedding tears as characters face emotional upheavals. Her husband—her constant companion—never forgets to carry along a tissue box, knowing it's as essential to their movie outings as the popcorn.

An ambivert by nature and a firm believer that kindness never goes out of style, Mamata is happily married and nearing her 20th year of marriage. Her home is filled with love, shared with her daughter, her supportive entrepreneur husband, and two loyal dogs, Cookie and Brownie. Much of her writing is shaped by these life experiences, which have taught her the resilience of love and the beauty in imperfection.

Mamata also shares her musings on Instagram under the pen name stringspoetry, where she connects with her readers and expresses her thoughts through poetry. *Seasons of Love* is a reflection of hope and strength, reminding readers that even in moments of loss, there's always more to life, and not all is lost.

Acknowledgment

My love for reading was sparked by my father, an avid reader who introduced me to books at age three. From Alice in Wonderland to Black Beauty, P.G. Wodehouse's Jeeves, and the thrillers of Agatha Christie and James Hadley Chase, he opened my eyes to the magic of stories and adventure. I also delved into the worlds of Charles Dickens and the mysteries of Sherlock Holmes, which ignited my passion for deduction.

A special thanks to my mother for patiently listening to my poetic musings, and to my sisters, one who endured my ramblings, the other my most honest critic.

To my husband, for being my constant and always standing by my side. To my daughter, for showering me with unconditional love and inspiration. To my Insta family, thank you for giving me the confidence to keep writing.

To my dear 7:00 a.m. or 8:00 p.m. "call me anytime" friend, thank you for always being there.Thank you, Poonam, for taking the time to read the draft, providing me with your insights, and pouring confidence into me. Thanks, Ramya, for being there for me.

Lastly, to all the friends and strangers who have read my work and motivated me to complete this project, thank you for joining me on this journey. The adventure, both the journey and the destination, has been truly enthralling because of you all.

Introduction to Seasons of Love

Love is rarely a straight path. It takes us through seasons—each one marked by its own storms, blossoms, and harvests. In *Seasons of Love*, I've poured my heart into the experiences and emotions that come with loving deeply, losing painfully, healing slowly, and eventually finding love again. These poems aren't just drawn from my life but are woven from stories I've witnessed, emotions I've absorbed from books and movies, and fragments of the lives around me.

The first part, **Winter: Echoes of a Broken Heart**, captures the raw, piercing cold of heartbreak. Love, once so vibrant, slowly fades into an unbearable silence, leaving behind only memories that ache. It is in this season that I confronted the deepest truths about loss of love and betrayal. These poems carry the weight of those heartbreaks—the scars that remain after trust is shattered.

As we move into **Spring-Summer: Healing with Hope**, the journey of self-recovery begins. Like nature's rebirth, this part reflects the delicate process of healing. These poems explore grief, self-love, and the rediscovery of hope. In this season, there is pain, yes—but there is also growth, resilience, and the courage to find myself again. Each verse is a reminder that, even in the darkest of times, we have the strength to rise, to heal, and to embrace the light of new beginnings.

Finally, in **Autumn: Fated Hearts,** love returns, not as a fleeting passion but as a steady, enduring force. After the heartbreak and healing, I found a love that felt destined—deep, respectful, and fulfilling. This section celebrates a love built on mutual growth, understanding, and the quiet moments of togetherness that truly matter. It's a love story where both individuals, having weathered their own storms, come together to create something unbreakable and lasting.

Seasons of Love is a reflection of the seasons we all go through in life. Through these poems, I hope to share not only the heartache but also the hope, the healing, and the beauty that comes when love finds its way back to us. May you, too, find solace, strength, and love in these words.

From heartbreak to healing, one season at a time.

Part 1

Season of Love
Winter: Echoes of a Broken Heart

In *Seasons of Love*, I invite you into a personal journey of love, loss, and betrayal. These poems are woven from my own experiences, as well as stories I've witnessed and emotions I've absorbed from books, movies, and fragments of life.

Love, once so vivid, slowly faded into haunting memories and the ache of unfulfilled dreams. As trust crumbled, I was forced to confront the painful truth that the love I believed in wasn't real.

Each poem echoes the heartache of realizing the person I loved wasn't who I thought they were. My heart is scarred by a love that never truly existed, and those scars are etched into every line.

Through these verses, I pour out the pain of broken trust and shattered dreams, but also the story of resilience—the journey of learning to let go and finding strength to move forward. I hope that in sharing these emotions, others who have faced loss and betrayal find solace in knowing they are not alone.

Echoes Of a Broken Heart

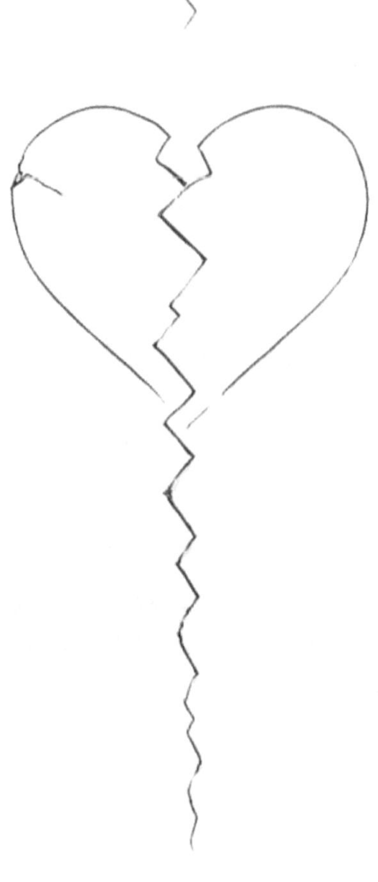

Epiphany

Grief consumed me, cloaking me in sorrow for the loss I thought I couldn't bear.

But beneath the pain, what hurt was the betrayal.

It wasn't just love lost, but trust shattered, and suddenly, grief became a mask for the lies that tore me apart.

Wave of Grief

Grief is like a wave,
She comes in highs and lows like the tide.
Wrapping you in a blanket of memories,
Warm, yet distant, like a fading dream.

She numbs your heart,
Filling it with despair and regret.
Leaving you forlorn,
Lost in melancholy.

All that remains are scattered shards of a heart
Never whole again.

The Shining Stars

Do the scars of pain fade,
Or do they become stars of grief
Lighting up the night sky?

Mamata Sampath

So Close Yet So Far

I have so many things to share
But then
The only thing that comes out of me
Is a sigh.
How did we get so far,
Staying so close?

So Close Yet So Far

Mosaic of Memories

All that is left of us is memories
As we could never have had a forever.

Mamata Sampath

Almost

We could have almost,
Almost had it all.
But then you left.

Far too Well

The truth unsettles,
So you found comfort
In a blanket of lies
Stitched so perfectly
I hardly noticed,
Until you wore it
Always....
Far too well.

Mamata Sampath

Lies

You lie, I believe.
You ignore, I accept.
Your love is gone,
But mine won't let go

Lost in Maybe

Maybe it was the wrong time,
Maybe the stars missed our wishes.
In all the maybes, I didn't see
We were never meant to be.

You and Me

You and me
Beautiful ruins
Always a history

You and Me

Us

24

I will walk the same road,
Stand under the same tree,
Thinking of you and the probability of us.

Mamata Sampath

Buried Bones

I dig up our memories
Like buried bones,
They don't decompose easily.
These memories of us,
They don't perish,
They linger, painting pain,
Of grief and betrayal

Matter's Most

You'll always remember
What matters most.
Somehow...
I was never on your
To remember list.

Us

I still weep
For an ending we were never meant to have.

Us

I still think of us,
But only in ifs and buts.

Outgrow

I tucked you in with love,
But like old clothes, you outgrew me.
Or was it I who outgrew you?

The Truth

Why make up stories
When the truth
Was more than enough?
To end it all.

Mamata Sampath

Why make up stories
When the truth

Love Mansion

You built a love mansion
On a foundation of lies
No wonder it crumbled,
As the ugly truth seeped in.

Wilted Flowers of Trust

If trust were something I could buy,
I'd have given it all to you.
But trust, like flowers, wilts,
And now nothing blooms between us.

Mamata Sampath

The Other Girl

I was always your "maybe,
"Never your "Forever,"
Always the other girl,
Never "The One."
A substitute, standing in love's shadow.

Fairy Tale—Not

We began like a fairy tale,
But ours didn't have a happily ever after.

The Story

It all depends
On who tells the story.
In yours,
I'm forever the villain,
No matter the truth

Love of Lies

All you spoke were lies,
And I knew it all along.
My mind screamed the truth,
Yet my heart found comfort in your words.

Mamata Sampath

Words of Woe

You said sorry,
But didn't mean it.
I said okay,
But didn't feel it.
Empty words exchanged,
And in silence, all seemed well.

Beyond Words

It was never what you said,
But how you made me feel.
The things left unsaid
Echoed louder than any promise.
Your actions spoke louder,
Revealing it all.

Mamata Sampath

Eyes Don't Lie

Your eyes gave away
What your lips guarded—Deceit.

Known Stranger

We spent every moment together,
Weaving dreams of silk and satin.
We laughed and cried as one,
Crafting memories from passing moments.
I believed we were soulmates,
Never realizing it wasn't the real you
But merely your silhouette.
I faltered in deciphering you,
As you wove a web of lies with precision.
Willingly, I became entangled—in the name of love.
Your deceit dissected my heart,
Like a surgeon's knife, sharp and exact,
Until I realized you were a known stranger all along.

Mamata Sampath

Wounded Words

I am wounded,
But not with blood.
My wounds bleed words,
For that's all that's left of us.

Broken Mirror

My heart is a shattered mirror,
I see myself in scattered pieces,
Never whole again.

More than your betrayal,
It was love itself,
That broke me.

If Only

If there's an afterlife,
Maybe we could be soulmates there.
If only...

Whenever You Said...

I died a million times
Knowing you lied
Whenever you said
I love you too

Part 2

Season of Love
Spring-Summer: From Heartbreak to Hope

A Journey Through Grief, Self-Love, and Healing

In this collection, I present the second chapter of my emotional journey—a chapter that moves through grief, self-care, and the delicate process of healing. These poems reflect not only the grief of lost love but the rediscovery of the self-amidst that pain. Each verse is a step toward self-love, resilience, and the slow but steady process of healing a broken heart.

As the grief fades, I begin to embrace a stronger version of myself, one shaped not just by pain but by resilience and hope. These poems carry the weight of sorrow but also the lightness of new beginnings, and I hope they resonate with anyone who has been through the complex process of healing.

This is a journey of remembering that, even in the darkest times, we all have the capacity to heal, to grow, and to love ourselves again. By sharing these emotions, I hope those who have felt the weight of loss and betrayal find comfort in knowing they are not alone. This is a shared path, and through these verses, we can all find solace, strength, and hope in healing.

From Heartbreak to Hope

Epiphany

I realized healing wasn't in the hands of those who hurt me but within myself. The love and peace I sought were always there, beneath grief and self-doubt.

Healing meant embracing the pain as part of my growth, allowing me to rebuild as someone stronger and wiser.

Denial

We have a choice:
Choke in denial
Or rise in acceptance.

Rampage of Rage

If grief and rage
Rampage
And burn you to ash,
Burn like a phoenix

Only to be born again,
To rise from the grief,
Better and stronger.

Sculpture and the Sculpted

You are
The sculptor
And the sculpture.

Your grief
Was the chisel
That shaped you
Into strength.

Mamata Sampath

You Deserve Better

And sometimes,
You must rescue
Yourself from you.
No one knows,
You deserve better
More than you.

Like the Moon

Maybe you're broken
And will never be whole again.
But can't we be like the moon,
With the wax and the wane?

Firefly

You
Faced your darkness
Like a firefly,
Lighting your way
And that is,
What survivors do.

Care

It's time
You cared for yourself,
The way the world moves on,
Caring only for itself.

Heal

Acceptance is courage
The strength to see
What is.
Only when you see,
Can you heal.

Moon Child

Like the moon
We will heal
In phases
Slow and steady

Mamata Sampath

Impermanence

Nothing lasts forever
Neither happiness, nor sorrow.
Impermanence is nature's law.
This too shall pass.

Circle of Life

Those petals were meant to fall.
Only after they wither
Can the bud bloom.

Light and Dark

Maybe you have to be in the dark
To appreciate the light

Let Yourself Hurt

Let yourself hurt,
Then let yourself heal.

Feel every crack,
Feel what's real.

Don't rush the pain,
Don't push it away.

Give it the time
To fade someday.

Feather Heart

I did something brave today
I finally cried.
It lightened my empty heart,
Like a feather.

Time

Give yourself love,
And give it time.
Even the rawest wounds will heal
Time heals best when given time.

Mamata Sampath

Trust the Climb

In the quiet moments,
Let yourself heal.

After storms have passed,
Allow the calm to feel real

The scars you carry,
They'll fade in time.

Just give yourself space,
And trust the climb.

A Better Tomorrow

Let me stitch that bleeding heart
With love and care,
With understanding and hope,
With kindness and patience.

It will be whole again,
Like daffodils in bloom,
Radiating hope for a better tomorrow.

Mamata Sampath

Self-Love and Care

You Deserve the Care
You give to others,
The same love
You pour on them.

Self-Love and Care

Dress-up

You always gave
What you never received
Love, kindness, and understanding.
It's time to tend your wounds,
Rather than dressing up others'.

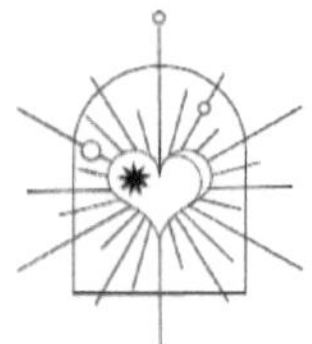

Save Yourself

You must save yourself.
A knight in shining armour
Is just a fairy tale.

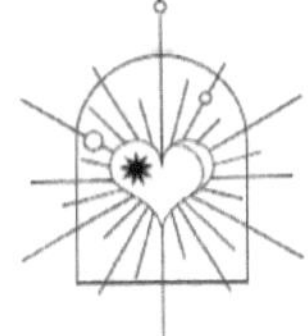

Re-discover

Only when you're lost
Can you truly discover.
Maybe it's time
To find the new you.

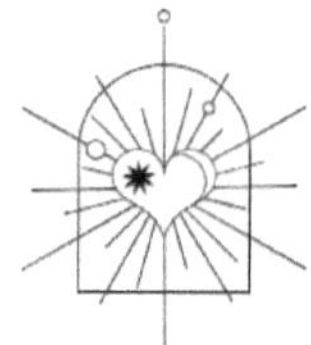

Survivor

You're stronger
Than you ever knew.
You survived the storm
Where others drowned.

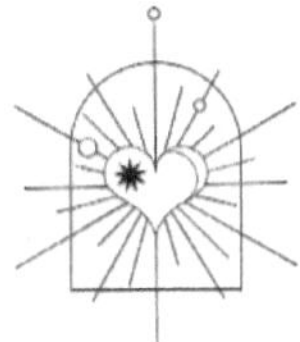

Warrior

The scars you bear
Aren't marks of failure,
But proof of the warrior in you
The one who didn't just survive,
But rose in glory, too.

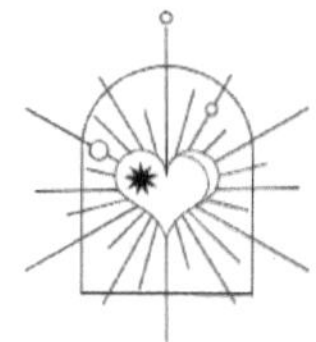

A Resilient Ocean

Be an ocean
Serene and magnificent,
Impregnable and resilient.
Through high tides and low,
Revel in your existence.

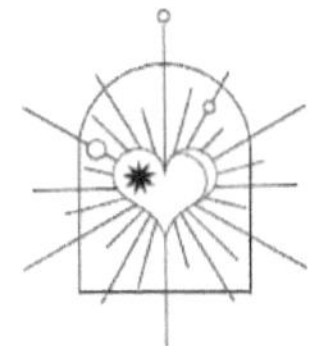

Metamorphosis

Believe in the magic of life.
The fragile caterpillar
Became a butterfly.
You too will find your wings,
In life's quiet metamorphosis.

Mamata Sampath

Oasis

Even the barren desert finds an oasis,
Why not wrap yourself
In kindness,
And feel its warmth?

The Sky and the Stars

The stars
Shine beautifully
In their imperfection.

The sky
Lives through another day,
Cloudy or bright.

So shall we
Continue to live,
Embracing our flaws.

Mamata Sampath

Road of Healing

Walk the road of healing,
Taking shade in faith.

Gather strength
From promising tomorrows.

And when you feel like giving up,
Let the stars of hope whisper,

"Just one more step, one more day,
And you shall arrive."

On Its Way

Everything
You've been waiting for,
All that you deserve,
Is already on its way to you.

Merry Song

No matter what,
Listen to your favorite song.
Dance to the beat,
For life is just
A merry tune... sometimes offbeat.

Part 3

Season of Love
Autumn: Fated Hearts

After navigating heartbreak and healing, the author steps into a new chapter—one marked by love, hope, and fulfilment. This phase reflects not only personal experiences but also stories from friends, books, and movies. In it, she finds her soulmate—someone who stands as an equal, complementing her journey toward self-discovery.

Together, they build a bond grounded in mutual respect and understanding. Matured and wiser, she realizes that love grows not through grand gestures but in the quiet moments of connection, patience, and unwavering support.

Life's ups and downs become a shared rhythm, filled with laughter and challenges they face together.

This journey reveals that real love transcends passion; it's about building a partnership where both individuals grow and flourish. Their bond, despite life's imperfections, is what truly matters—a story of enduring love, where forgiveness, respect, and togetherness forge a forever.

Fated Hearts

Epiphany

Love, in its purest form, is never perfect

It is patient and kind, finding strength in our imperfections.

Together, we stand, not as halves, but as whole souls intertwined,

Facing the world hand in hand, with respect, trust, and unwavering faith.

And in this love, I've found everything I never knew I needed.

Mamata Sampath

Fated Hearts

We were meant to be,
So our paths crossed,
Not by chance,
But by destiny.
Fated hearts,
Interwove
We are
Where we were always meant to be,
Together.

Destiny

Maybe it was the shooting stars
And the fireflies,
That gently lit the path
And led me to you.
The night whispered secrets
Only hearts could understand,
As sparks danced in the sky
And fate took my hand.
I wandered through the dark,
Lost in endless dreams,
Until your light appeared
Soft and warm, like moonlit beams.
Was it chance or destiny,
A silent wish, a quiet sigh?
In the glow of falling stars,
I found love beneath the sky.

                                                    Mamata Sampath

Conspiracy of the Cosmos

It was destiny,
Divine providence,
Conspiracy of the cosmos
That we must meet.
Like the ocean meets his tides,
Like an oasis finds her desert,
Like woven threads in intricate fabric,
Our fates intertwined.
And from that moment on,
The rest was history.

Matter of Time

The universe had a plan—
You and I, destined to meet,
To fall in love.
It was only a matter of time.

Mamata Sampath

I Still Remember

I still remember
How I felt
The first time I met you
A thumping heart,
Eyes locked on you,
And a smile
That never left my face.

Not at First Sight

It wasn't love at first sight,
But something slow and gentle,
Like the blooming of buds,
The first snowflakes of December,
The midsummer drizzle of rain,
Or a soft autumn breeze.
It wasn't love at first sight,
But something slow and gentle,
YOU and Me.

Mamata Sampath

The Storm

You were the sunshine
That calmed the storm within.

The Storm

Lost Forever

My heart skips a beat,
Strums a merry tune,
Catching a fleeting glimpse of you.
Butterflies flutter deep within,
You, a taste of stardust,
A sweet ache in my heart.
You, my unabashed love—
Say something, please.
At least give me back
My stolen heart piece.

Mamata Sampath

Verses in a Timeless Song

You and me
Chaos and order,
Rhythm and rhyme,
A dance of opposites,
Yet we find balance,
In every beat,
In every pause,
Like verses in a timeless song.

Piece of Art

With you, I am whole again.
My broken pieces look beautiful,
Just like art pieced together
With love, understanding, and care.

Piece of Art

Mamata Sampath

Where I Found Home

I sought solace in climbing mountains,
In the rhythm of the waves,
In sunsets and sunrises,
In the melody of music.
Yet I found it all at once,
In your embrace.

YOU

The world broke me,
But you, my universe,
Put me back together
With the magic of love.

Mamata Sampath

You Remembered

You remembered
What I had forgotten
A happy me.
Somehow,
You brought her back,
Made me whole again.

Journey with You

I embraced life
With love,
Because you are now
A part of it.

In Silent Sync

Time stood still
As I sat by your side.
Our heartbeats in perfect sync,
In silence,
We found everything
we'd been searching for.

The Root of Us

We gave what we sought—
Deeper than love,
Stronger than desire.
Respect—
That is what made us
Who we are today.

Mamata Sampath

US

"It will always be us,"
You said,
When we first met.
It still stands true
Till date.

Our Moments

Your lopsided smile,
The wink,
The footsies—
They have a home in my heart forever.
Our moments.

Mamata Sampath

Relationship Blend

A relationship is a delicate blend
Respect, trust, love, and hope.
It must be brewed with patience
To flourish and grow.

To Love

To love is
To embrace everything—
The good, the bad,
And all that lies between.

Mamata Sampath

New Me

I smile, staring at the walls,
Humming a song I never knew,
Wearing colors I never dared.
Is this the new me,
Or is it all of you in me?

Just the Way, I Need You

I want to grow old with you,
Laugh at your clumsy ways,
Clean up your messes,
And hold close the knowing
That you'll always need me,
Just as I need you.

Mamata Sampath

Love

Through mistakes,
Through fights and arguments,
We'll still stand close—
You and me,
Unbreakable,
Whole.
For that is love.

My Happily Ever After

You are...
The color in my rainbow,
The full moon in my darkest night,
The heartbeat in my song.
You are...
My forever, my always.

Mamata Sampath

Perfectly Imperfect

There are days we fight,
And days I cry,
But in the end, together,
We face it all—
And that's what truly matters
In our perfectly imperfect life.

A Lifetime of Us

You always meant
What you said,
A lifetime of us.
Through happiness and joy,
Our miseries and mistakes,
My chaos and your order,
My rage, your calm.
Your forgetfulness,
And my never forgetting a thing.
You always meant
What you said,
A lifetime of us.

Mamata Sampath

For Every Lifetime

This lifetime, and every lifetime after,
I just want it to be "us."

All Over Again

I still miss you
Every morning and night,
When you're not around.
And each time, I fall in love with you
All over again.

Mamata Sampath

Fell in Love

Not in shine and glitter,
But in trust and warmth,
You and I
Fell in love.

Our Tomorrow

I'm glad I have you.
Together, we'll face it all.

Mamata Sampath

End Note

As I reflect on this journey through love, loss, and healing, I realize that every heartbreak, every moment of joy, and every whisper of hope has shaped me into who I am today.

Love is never a single chapter—it's a story that unfolds, season by season, bringing with it lessons that heal us, even in the quietest moments.

I've learned that the beauty of love isn't just in finding it, but in growing through its seasons. From the cold silence of heartbreak to the warmth of rediscovery, love teaches us that healing is always possible, and hope always returns.

Thank you for walking with me through these seasons.

www.ingramcontent.com/pod-product-compliance
Lightning Source LLC
Chambersburg PA
CBHW031306130726
47988CB00007B/2750